Robin Hardin, one of C
heart deeply with her willi
ence is better to Him than s
doing both. In her writing
one so gifted that she is abl
the Holy Spirit is able to util
the while she seems to live at Jesus' feet, like Mary chose to do.

Not only are those in her presence blessed by the likeness she bears to Lazarus' sisters, but they also get to witness a modern day "Davida," the effeminate of David, the psalmist and king who danced before the Lord…abandoning self for unrestrained service to God in the dance. How *grace*-fully Robin dances before the Lord of lords and King of kings in the anointing of His Holy Spirit! Yet another name? I believe so. I'd also have to call Robin Hardin "Grace"—God's beautiful "Amazing Grace."

Jeannie C. Riley
"Harper Valley PTA"
Recording Artist

It's funny to think about arguing with God, yet we all do it from time to time. This book points out the reality of our insecurities, our thoughts, our fears. And then it happens: Through reading about Robin's life experiences, somehow we are enabled to move from the place of arguing with God to submitting. This book is a must-read for anyone who has decided to be obedient to God!

Monica Schmelter

Whenever I've wanted to accomplish something big—or to make changes in my life—I have never done strictly "academic" research or relied on "classroom theories." I've always looked for someone who has "been there and done that"—and, for that matter, "been there and done that, very well"! That's exactly what Robin helps us do in this book. Her real life experiences and her "arguments" with God are captivating—they can take you from a place of insecurity to a place of freedom in Christ.

Joe Schmelter

Pastor Joe and Monica Schmelter
Gateway of Hope International Ministries

I love to read the stories of Robin Hardin. I will go to a quiet place or wait until I go to bed at night to read Robin's stories. They give my heart an ounce of laughter and my soul a ton of comfort, which always makes for a good night's sleep!

Patti Jo Brayfield
CMT (Country Music Television)
Writer / Producer

With honesty and grace, Robin Hardin will lead you along her journey through spiritual- and self-doubt into faith and self-discovery. She illustrates how, through faith and love, it is possible to overcome the "demons" of self-absorption and prejudgment and discover the sometimes-hidden beauty and gifts in one's self and others.

Dr. Mitzi Wood-Von Mizener
Clinical Psychologist

I have known Robin for many years, and she has always been an inspiration to me. She is the "rock" at our workplace. If anyone is in need of prayer, they always find Robin to be their intercessor.

Her stories, which are an extension of her walk with God, serve as an encouragement to us all. She has a gift for writing about her heartfelt emotions that will move you to laughter and tears and challenge you to a closer walk.

Diana Grubbs
MTV Networks
Post Production Coordinator

Dear Robin,

Thank you for sharing your short stories with me. I would share the stories with my coworkers, and they would want to keep my copy. Because I am not an avid reader, it was good to find something I wanted to read. There is such life in your writing that it drew me right into the experience. I was able to see and feel it as if I were there. Robin, you shared your true-life experience with an honesty and transparency that was deeply therapeutic to me. Again, thank you so much.

Anita Jones
Nurse

An honest, candid, and vulnerable account of one sister's odyssey in walking with God through her insecurities—and finding peace, joy, security, and significance in Jesus Christ.

Tom Clark
District Sales Manager
Fujifilm

Walking, Talking, Debating and Arguing with GOD

Selections on Overcoming the Insecurities and Fears in Our Lives

ROBIN HARDIN

ACW Press
Phoenix, Arizona 85013

Walking, Talking, Debating and Arguing with God
Copyright ©2002 Robin Hardin
All rights reserved

Cover Design by Alpha Advertising
Interior design by Pine Hill Graphics

Packaged by ACW Press
5501 N. 7th Ave., #502
Phoenix, Arizona 85013
www.acwpress.com
The views expressed or implied in this work do not necessarily reflect those of ACW Press. Ultimate design, content, and editorial accuracy of this work is the responsibility of the author(s).

Library of Congress Cataloging-in-Publication Data
(Provided by Quality Book, Inc.)

Hardin, Robin.
    Walking, talking, debating, and arguing with God / by
Robin Hardin. -- 1st ed.
    p. cm.
    ISBN 1-892525-88-7

    1. Christian life. 2. Bashfulness. 3. Anxiety.
4. Fear--Social aspects. I. Title.

BV4501.2.H37 2002   248.4
                            QBI33-568

All rights reserved. No part of this book may be reproduced, stored in a retrieval system, or transmitted in any form or by any means–electronic, mechanical, photocopying, recording, or otherwise–without prior permission in writing from the copyright holder except as provided by USA copyright law.

Printed in the United States of America.

Dedicated to my granddaughter Jimi.

My prayer is that you never lose the special relationship you have with Jesus.

From the Mouth of Babes

Three-year-old Jimi: "Grandma, you know what? Jesus talks to me when I'm outside."

Grandma: "He does? That's wonderful, honey."

Jimi put her finger to her lips and whispered:

"Yeah, I have to be real quiet so I can hear Jesus when He talks to me."

Table of Contents

Shy and Slain 11

A Joyful Noise 21

Jesus Walk 25

Attitude Adjustment..................... 33

Butterfly 45

Promises, Bargains, and Covenants 63

Command Performance................... 81

Stretches, Sit-ups, and Weights 93

Introduction

This book was not designed to preach or teach a doctrine. It's a collection of personal experiences encountered on my daily walks with Christ. Every chapter is written in short story form, making random selection an option. However, when read cover to cover, the awesome work of God is laid out as He planned. This writing originated as a special gift for my granddaughter. After I'd gone to be with Jesus, she'd have my spiritual journal to comfort her. Over time I realized others could benefit from my testimony as well. I pray you are encouraged, entertained, enlightened, and enriched by it.

Robin Hardin

Chapter One

Shy and Slain

November 12, 1997

Growing up I was oppressively shy. The fact that my family moved at least once every school year contributed greatly to my phobia of people. Up to the time I was a sophomore in high school, only once did we spend two Christmases in the same house. Being the new kid every year, and knowing I'd move before the year ended, friendships seemed a waste of time.

I may actually hold the world's record for the fewest of questions answered during a primary education. I managed to attend school from first grade to twelfth without answering a single teacher's question. From the time I started school at six years old until I graduated at age seventeen, I raised my hand one time. It was the most embarrassing experience of life up to that point. My hand was raised, but I didn't answer the question. I didn't even answer the teacher as he repeatedly asked why I would raise my hand and then not say a word.

To this day, I feel he set me up. He told the class he was going to call someone who looked like they didn't know the answer. Not willing to take the chance of him saying my name aloud, I had only one option. I raised my hand, hoping he'd call on someone else. Apparently he was shocked that my hand was in the air and addressed the question to me. The blood rushed to my face and my hand slowly dropped to my side as I heard my name called. The sound of my name being spoken out loud in front of others put my stomach in knots. I'm sure he said it only once, but it echoed over and over in my brain. For what seemed like an eternity, I sat motionless, staring down at my desk. My heart felt as if it would burst right out of my chest. The students around me were probably vibrated by its rapid thumping. Knowing everyone was looking at me, I dared not shift my gaze. My debilitating shyness made me physically sick and caused me to miss school the next day.

Everyone has awkward childhood experiences. Normal situations were worsened by my painful shyness.

Shy and Slain

I used to walk down the hall between classes and never make eye contact with students as we passed. More than once my lunch period was spent hiding in the restroom, to avoid walking into the cafeteria alone.

One day in high school the girl I hung around with became ill and went home early. Unfortunately, she left before lunch. The restrooms were being monitored because students had been caught smoking. If I were to be found hiding in there I'd be accused of smoking. This presented a major dilemma. I was faced with the decision of eating lunch all by myself or risking my restroom retreat. Out of desperation, I called to have Mom pick me up because I honestly wasn't feeling well. The thought of asking to sit at a table with someone made me sick to my stomach.

As a child, being forced from my comfort zone was traumatic. The slightest change of routine caused me undue stress. I found refuge with my family. Time spent with them at home and at church was precious to me. I looked forward to church services because I felt safe and secure while in the house of God. Being raised Pentecostal I've witnessed various spiritual signs and wonders. Seeing saints speak in heavenly languages and being slain in the spirit are common scenes in the churches I've attended through the years.

I'm completely comfortable with others being blessed with a touch from God. At times, I've felt a tinge of envy because of their lack of inhibition. I could only speculate how free they must feel to be unconcerned with the opinion of others. That concept is totally foreign to me. Being able to see people receive such anointing allowed me to be blessed as well. I was happy living vicariously through their spiritual experiences. Until recently, I have not exactly desired the same for myself. After all, someone may look at me. I was forty years old before I ever raised my hand to praise the Lord (probably suppressed trauma from my history class so many years ago).

One day in church, we were singing a song about bringing a sacrifice of praise unto the Lord. Our praise and worship leader admitted how sometimes lifting one's hands can be difficult and embarrassing. By surrendering our insecure feelings and raising our hands toward heaven, we're making a sacrifice. Knowing I wasn't the only person on earth having trouble with this simple act enabled me to face that fear head on. Well, almost head on. I raised one of my hands about as high as my chin, which was a giant step for me.

I was most definitely bringing a sacrifice to the Lord. The longer my hand was elevated, the heavier it became. It took energy to support my now seemingly fifty-pound limb. With my eyes closed, I imagined that everyone in the entire church had quit worshiping and were just watching me. The thought crossed my mind to withdraw in a hurry, but I decided against any sudden movement. While trying to figure out how to get out of this situation, my arm started to go numb. It felt paralyzed. Recalling a quote from childhood, I

Shy and Slain

thought, *Oh no! What if it stays like this? How will I explain that one?*

My sacrifice was only offered for the duration of one song. The intention was to offer a sacrifice of praise, but the result was something far less. I was no longer singing, nor worshiping. My focus had shifted from Christ back down to me. Just like Peter walking on water, as long as his eyes were on Jesus, he was fine. Once his focus shifted to himself, he began to drown. I too was beginning to drown in my overactive imagination.

Trying to appear as inconspicuous as possible, I lowered my hand as the song ended. For the remainder of the service, I concentrated on the reason I'd attended church in the first place. I was there to worship my Savior, and to glorify His name. Church is where I'm fed God's Word, and my relationship with Him is strengthened.

A year later, I'm finally able to raise my hand while worshiping. Raising both hands, however, is still somewhat of a problem. I'm not sure why I'm afraid two hands will draw any more attention than one. I'm not sure why I think anyone cares if I raise my hands or not. I tell myself that if everyone else is here for the right reason, they'll be worshiping. If they have their eyes on Jesus, they're not looking at me. That logic sounds good to the realistic portion of my brain. Admittedly, I'm having some difficulty with convincing the portion of my brain in which my self-consciousness is so deeply rooted.

As an adult, I've learned to control much of my shyness. Obviously, I have a long way to go. Being so self-conscious greatly hinders areas of my life. Sometimes I don't allow myself to experience situations that would prove profitable to my emotional and spiritual growth.

Many times at the altar, the Holy Spirit is so strong people lose control of their bodies and collapse to the floor. This phenomenon is referred to as being slain in the spirit. As a teenager, my sister used to spend time at the altar in prayer. If someone next to her was receiving an anointing, she'd brush up against him or her, in hopes some of it would rub off. She used to pray that God would "zap" her. I, on the other hand, would pray that God would please let me remain standing. I wanted to be in control of my actions at all times. Besides, it was enough of a strain for me to force myself out of my pew to make that long trip to the altar. Eventually, I started sitting closer to the front of the church. This greatly reduced the distance from my pew to the altar.

It takes a strong person to respond to an altar call. It's much easier to just stay sitting comfortably in your seat. Otherwise, you have to excuse yourself for stepping on people's feet as you cross in front of them to get to the aisle. That walk down the aisle is a long, lonely walk. You keep looking straight ahead and don't make eye contact. Finally, you reach your destination. All of a sudden you feel the gaze of the congregation hot against the back of your neck. Then you go through the whole mental checklist. Are your shoes dirty? Is your zipper zipped, and buttons buttoned? Are you having a bad hair day? Does your backside look fat?

One particular Wednesday night, altar call changed my life forever. I'd learned earlier that a friend of mine had taken his own life. Hurting and confused, I was searching for answers. I knew Jesus promised us peace and comfort through the Holy Spirit. For the first time, I was unconcerned with the thoughts of others as I went forward for prayer. Not once did I worry about my appearance from the back. I needed a touch from the Comforter, and nothing was going to distract me.

Pastor was praying for individuals as the congregation softly sang praises. I felt as if I were the only person there. No longer was I aware of my surroundings. I had pressed through and was standing in the presence of the Almighty. I had captured God's attention, and certainly wasn't going to let it slip through my fingers. He was healing my soul, taking away my pain in the midst of tragedy. Christians often use the term "prayed through." After years of attending church and praying, I'd finally prayed through.

To this day, I have no idea how long I stood at the altar that night. Neither can I explain the power of the Almighty. I can tell you that a sweet peace swept through my spirit. The pain I'd endured seconds earlier

Walking, Talking, Debating and Arguing with God

had been divinely replaced with unspeakable joy. For a moment I wondered how my spirit could feel so light under such awful circumstances. Not only was I comforted, I was actually happy. I soon realized it's impossible to be sad while standing in the awesome presence of God.

At this point I could no longer hear Pastor or the singing. I was completely consumed by the Holy Spirit. A miraculous cleansing was being performed within my soul. Feeling like I was awakening from a deep, restful sleep, my eyes slowly opened. It took a few seconds to focus and get my bearings. The first thing I saw was the ceiling. Confused, I looked first to my left and then right. There were legs on either side of me. Beyond one pair of legs I could see someone lying on the floor as if they were taking a nap. Judging by the peaceful expression on their face, they were obviously experiencing that same restful sleep from which I had just awoken.

It seemed odd that I didn't have to look down in order to see this person on the floor. As a matter of a fact, we were at eye level to one another. How could that be? I was standing at the altar. I don't remember anyone praying over me or touching me. I remember walking to the altar and standing in prayer. Wait just a minute. I'm not standing. I'm lying on the floor in the middle of church, right here in front of God and everybody! How did I get down here? It finally occurred to me that I had been slain in the spirit. How did this happen? I wasn't praying for this. I certainly didn't see this coming. No warning at all, I just opened my eyes and realized I was horizontal!

God didn't ask permission to take control of my physical body. He had my permission to anoint my soul, and to bless my spirit. Those are safe touches from above, because other people in the room can't see them. This, however, was visible to everyone there. Had God asked me first, I would have refused to surrender my will.

Thank you, Jesus, for loving me in spite of my ignorance. Thank you for blessing me beyond my wildest dreams. Thank you for taking me to levels which my self-consciousness would otherwise limit me.

From the Mouth of Babes

Teacher: "Jesus told the disciples He had to leave them so He could send them a comforter. Who can tell me what the Comforter was that Jesus was talking about?"

Kelsie: "Oh! I know I know. Please call on me!"

Teacher: "Kelsie is new and has never answered any questions yet. Let's give her a turn."

Kelsie: (puffed up with pride) "It's a blanket."

Chapter Two

A Joyful Noise

May 17, 1998

If ever I had the slightest doubt about God's ability to use His people, today it vanished forever. We had a special singer in the church service that became a willing vessel through which God was truly glorified.

I thought perhaps I heard wrong when Pastor Joe introduced Brother Bobby as our special guest soloist for that day's service. Brother Bobby happens to sit behind me in church. At times I have to stop singing when his voice travels within hearing range. Not being a strong singer myself, I tend to follow anyone singing

Walking, Talking, Debating and Arguing with God

near me. It would not be very pleasant for the rest of the congregation if many of us started to sing in unison with Brother Bobby.

Bobby is a devoted, loyal man of God. He collects the offering for both Sunday school and Church. He is our official timekeeper, ringing the bell signifying the end of Sunday school. He has the responsibility of maintaining the attendance count and handing out the weekly bulletin. If someone misses a service, they will almost certainly receive a phone call during the week with Bobby sincerely telling them they were missed. In many areas, he is wonderfully talented. Unfortunately, singing is not one of them.

The entire church watched in silence as our dear brother made his way to the platform. He stands about five feet five inches tall. His two front teeth are missing, and he is prematurely gray. One leg is several inches shorter than the other causing an obvious limp. There he stood in his black western boots, black polyester dress slacks pulled up high to his chest, and his contemporary Christian T-shirt. His hands shook as he held the microphone. However I think that's normal for him, because he didn't appear to be the least bit nervous. On the contrary, he stood straight and proud. He was proud to be in the house of the Lord preparing to sing a song of praise to his Savior.

Perhaps I was the most nervous person in the congregation. Bobby's wife was sitting directly behind me, and his daughter directly in front. Any adverse reaction

A Joyful Noise

from me would not go undetected. To avoid a case of the proverbial giggles in church, I felt the safest thing for me to do would be to close my eyes. His inability to find a key and stick with it is less than comfortable, even to my untrained ear. I couldn't help but wonder how our praise and worship members and other musicians would bear this event.

It was a pleasant surprise to hear that the sound track had good loud backup singers. My strategy was to concentrate on the music and vocals on the track. As I sat there with my eyes closed, I managed to listen to the words of the song instead of how it sounded. The song was about Jesus paying a debt He didn't owe. One line mentions a new song we'll sing when we get to heaven. The angels will have to be silent because they won't be able to sing about the redemption we've received.

During the chorus, it seemed as if maybe Bobby actually understood the idea of carrying a tune. Much to my astonishment, I was beginning to enjoy what I was listening to. I opened my eyes to make sure it was still Bobby singing. For the first time, I read the words printed on his T-shirt, "Make a joyful noise unto the Lord." How fitting, his voice may not be polished and melodic, but it was joyful. He wasn't there to entertain me, or anybody else in that room. He was singing from his heart, giving all he had to glorify the Lord.

As I closed my eyes once again, I felt a tear slide slowly down my cheek. It wasn't a tear of pain as I had sarcastically thought previously. Much to my surprise, Brother Bobby's solo had been a blessing to me. The number of eyes being wiped with hankies and dabbed with tissues indicated the majority of the congregation was sharing this blessing.

What a humbling experience—my arrogant thoughts toward another had become judgment on my own behavior. I was getting another hard lesson on humility. As Brother Bobby finished his song, God spoke to me loud and clear. The words seemed to rip through the inner chambers of my soul. "The least of you shall be great, and the great shall be least."

After repenting and begging forgiveness, I began to give God praise. I was thankful for the conviction laid upon me, and for His blessing. Hopefully, sometime in the near future, Brother Bobby will stand before us and once again make a joyful noise unto the Lord.

From the Mouth of Babes

Young Christopher had not been raised in church. So when his grandmother started taking him to Sunday school, he learned some songs he had not heard at home. On the way to Sunday school he sang a new song for his grandmother:

"Jesus loves me this I know, I love Rock and Roll, 'cause the Bible tells me so."

Chapter Three

Jesus Walk

May 30, 1998

Here in the South, the last Saturday in May is typically pleasant, spring-like weather. Today, however, was in the mid 90s and the humidity was unbearable. It was not exactly the perfect day for a mile-long walk down the middle of Main Street, yet more than eighty people joined together and did just that.

Our small country town was participating in an annual "Jesus Walk." This is a worldwide event where Christians all over the globe take a stand for Jesus.

Walking, Talking, Debating and Arguing with God

Compared to the hundreds of walkers hosted by some large cities, eighty doesn't sound like much. When that many men, women and children gathered together to praise the Lord in our quaint town square it was rather impressive.

Events such as this prove that Christians come in many races, ages, and religions. Several denominations were represented, with pastors and members from area churches participating. One pastor brought members of his congregation from a neighboring town to join the celebration of Jesus. People showed up in every kind of vehicle you could imagine, from rusted out pickup trucks to shiny new Cadillacs. Some were dressed in cut-off jeans and T-shirts, while others sported casual wear and neatly pressed cotton shirts.

Young and old alike lifted the name of Jesus. Adults carried brilliant satin banners trimmed in gold, glorifying their Savior. These magnificent banners softly rippling in the breeze with their streamers dancing did not overshadow the ones carried by the children. They had worked hard painting and gluing to create their own felt masterpieces.

Even more beautiful were the precious, rosy-cheeked faces of the children, their bright eyes filled with excitement. Tiny hands clutched pint-size banners, and little legs took two steps to every one of ours in order to keep up. As the sun reflected the miniature beads of perspiration, their soft skin sparkled like diamonds. They were laughing and having a good time, unaware of the fact that they were actually solders in the Lord's army.

Music played and songs were sung as the parade of Christians slowly descended down Main Street headed for the square. Along the way, cars honked and passengers cheered. Local merchants stepped out to the curb for a closer look. It wasn't long before the heat from the pavement radiated through the soles of our shoes. The exhaust from passing motorists added to the rising temperature as the sun never seemed to find a cloud behind which it could hide.

I began thinking about the many other ways I could be spending my Saturday afternoon, all of which included air conditioning and perhaps a nice tall glass of lemonade. About that time, I came to an alley that ran between two buildings. At the end of the alley I could see the railroad tracks and someone standing beyond them. The salt from my sweat was stinging my eyes, making it necessary to blink a couple of times in order to focus on the figure in the distance.

Standing all alone, in the hot sun, was an elderly lady watching the "Jesus Walk." Probably someone's grandmother on her way to town, she had on a dress and carried her purse close to her body. I didn't see a car nearby, so I don't know how far she may have walked to witness this event. A lump formed in my throat as I saw her watching and waving to us. Seeing her standing for so long under the same rays of sun as I was suffering through inspired me to continue on with a renewed spirit. She was oblivious to the fact that her presence had touched at least one heart.

Once the parade reached its destination, the pastors from each church represented led the crowd in prayer. Even one of our local politicians proclaimed his faith and openly praised God with us. Prayers were sent heavenward for our community, our state, our country, and our world.

I held my camera to my face in an attempt to capture the moment forever. Peering through the viewfinder, preparing my shot, it was as if I was seeing this group of people for the first time. No longer were they just a hot, tired crowd. They were loving, compassionate, individual creations of the Almighty.

There were babies sleeping in strollers, and elderly men and women who must have arrived by car, being too old to have walked. There were skin tones that ranged from milky white to midnight black, and every shade in between. Everyone was standing side by side; some held hands and shared hugs. There were no lines dividing first class from second. There were no seats, so no one was sitting in the back.

These individuals were coexisting as the Creator intended, equal in every way. They were in one accord as they stood and prayed to one God. Some heads were bowed low; some faces gazed skyward as if looking into the face of Jesus. Hands were reaching high into the air, while others were folded with fingers intertwined. The Bible says God inhabits the praises of His people. His presence was certainly felt in the middle of town square today.

After a final prayer, the unusual praise and worship service was dismissed. The crowd split off into smaller groups for the mile-long trek back to their cars. About half a mile later, I began to sink right back into my pity party. The sun was directly overhead now, causing the temperature to rise ever closer toward one hundred degrees. Tired and overheated, my thirst and hunger were in competition to bring me to my knees. I couldn't walk as fast as I would have liked because I had my four-year-old granddaughter with me.

Up ahead was a man walking by himself. His steps were slower and seemingly more laborious than the other walkers were. At first I thought perhaps his slow pace was due to his thin, frail frame, lacking any obvious muscle tone. As the distance between us shortened, I could see he was several years my senior. Judging by the thickness of his glasses, he suffered some degree of vision impairment as well. I walked with him a while in case he needed assistance. The manner in which he held his side indicated he was experiencing some pain.

We exchanged smiles, and he began to share with me how much he enjoyed the day. The singing and reading of the Scriptures had anointed his soul. He said the blessing he received had made his struggle worth every step, although his doctor would not be thrilled that he had participated. After all, it was only three days prior that his appendix had been removed.

Walking, Talking, Debating and Arguing with God

Boy, did I ever get an attitude adjustment. I'm probably half this man's age, healthy, and have all my original parts, including my appendix. Three times a week, I lift weights. On average, I walk about a mile, four or five days a week. Of course, my exercise routine takes place in the comfort of my own home, with lots of ice water and the air conditioning cranked. I suddenly felt ashamed of my selfish, silent whining. It was my choice to join this walk, yet I was acting as if it were a huge sacrifice.

God has a way of putting us in our place when needed. He used someone who appeared weak in the eyes of man to show a display of strength, which comes from the Holy Spirit. The spiritual "thump on the head" I received today was definitely deserved. I decided to stop feeling sorry for myself and get on down the road. I picked up my pace and gave my granddaughter a piggyback ride so she could have some relief.

After a few blocks, someone from my church stopped their truck and gave us a ride. Upon reaching my car, I drove back down the road looking for the frail walker. I wanted to give him the chance to rest his weary body. His sweet spirit had prompted me to count my blessings, and I wanted to offer him something in return. I never found him, so I never even got the chance to thank him. Surely he will be honored by his Heavenly Father for his spirit of joy and his willingness to take a stand (or walk) for Jesus.

Jesus Walk

Later, relaxing in the cool comfort of my home, my brother came over for a visit. I told him about the "Jesus Walk." Jokingly, he asked if that was anything like a cakewalk. "What do you do?" he said. "Do you walk around in a circle, and when the music stops, the winner gets Jesus?" I thought about that analogy. I guess it was somewhat like a cakewalk. We all walked until the music stopped. The difference was that there were no losers. We were all winners, because we had Jesus.

From the Mouth of Babes

The class was looking through the church photo album.

Teacher: "Most of you know Brother Kevin played the part of Jesus in the Easter play."

Jimi: "Where are Mr. Kevin's glasses?"

Teacher: "He removed his glasses because Jesus didn't wear glasses."

Jimi: "Oh yea, Jesus only wore glasses when he needed to read something."

Chapter Four

ATTITUDE ADJUSTMENT

April 1999

My sister Bambi wanted Mom and me to go with her to a women's conference her church was sponsoring. When she first mentioned it a few months ago, a "women only" weekend sounded like a fun time. As the designated weekend drew near, the whole idea seemed less than exciting. To be honest, I was trying to find an excuse to stay home. I've never been to Bambi's church, and wouldn't know anyone attending the conference. I am, by nature, a homebody and prefer to spend weekends with my husband, Gary.

It was Friday evening and Gary had only been home from work a few minutes. On most evenings we fix dinner together and share the events of the day at the table. Tonight, instead of helping with dinner, I begrudgingly threw some clothes into a suitcase. Grabbing my purse, I kissed him good-by and told him I loved him. Disgusted, I grumbled, "This conference better be good!" Those were my last words before leaving my house.

In my heart I knew a weekend trip to the mountains with my mom and sister could be a blast. But I was determined to roll around in my misery a while longer. It was a four-hour drive to the hotel where the conference was being held. I passed the time as the guest of honor of a well-planned pity party.

Because of Bambi's work schedule, we weren't able to leave home as early as originally planned. So we were late before we started. One the way, we missed a turn and drove nearly fifty miles beyond our intended destination. When we finally arrived, most people didn't realize we were late. They had already gone to their rooms to go to bed! It was just as well, since I was in no mood to mingle. However, I had paid money for this retreat and wanted to get every penny's worth. Being late is my absolute pet peeve. Therefore, this situation just added fuel to my fire.

As my attitude went from bad to worse I noticed a couple women painting some kind of small craft item. On a table were a few small butterfly pins and colorful

Attitude Adjustment

paints. One of the women cheerfully suggested we decorate one as a souvenir. I'm not much of a jewelry wearer and under the circumstances was feeling far less than creative. The last thing I wanted to do at the moment was color. And of all things, why a butterfly? They're so light and airy, and happy. Nevertheless, I had purchased one of the silly pins with my registration fee. Besides, I could take it home and give it to my six-year-old granddaughter.

As soon as we finished our craft, Bambi, Mom, and I went to our room. I desperately needed a good night's sleep. Surely, the dawning of another day would shed new light on my outlook. It turned out that a good night's sleep was not in my immediate future. Just as I was about to crawl into bed, an unbelievably sharp pain shot through my jaw. The crown on one of my teeth had come off exposing the nerve. It hurt to talk. It hurt to breathe. I tried not to breathe, but it hurt to hold my breath. This was not exactly a mood booster.

The best thing about my situation at this point was the fact that Bambi was with me. Not only is she my sister, she is also my dental hygienist. She instructed me to lie down on the bed. I hung my head over the side so she could look into my mouth. Taking the crown in her fingers she performed a couple of trial fittings to determine which way it was supposed to go. The pressure of that crown against my raw nerve was the most pain I had ever experienced. Unfortunately, that record-breaking pain was soon to be surpassed. We needed to put something in the crown to make it stay in place until I could get back home. The only thing available in that hotel room was spearmint toothpaste. Bambi turned the crown upside down between her finger and thumb. She filled the inside with toothpaste to act as a bonding agent.

With a compassionate voice, she said, " I'm gonna do this as fast as possible because it's going to hurt." I asked, "Aren't you supposed to say I'm going to experience some discomfort?" The answer I received was, "This isn't going to be uncomfortable. It's gonna hurt." She handed me a pillow to squeeze and said, "Ready?" I only thought I was ready. My fingernails practically bored holes in that pillow as pain shot through my whole body. My leg was involuntarily kicking like a little puppy when you scratch its belly. Tears were flowing uncontrollably. Since I was lying on my back, they ran out of my eyes and into my ears. Once I was able to sit up, I took several Advil and tried to get some sleep. My last conscious thought before drifting off was, "I knew this trip was a bad idea. I knew I should've stayed home."

Early the next morning we dressed and went to the conference room for breakfast. My idea of breakfast is a bowl of unsweetened cereal and a piece of toast without butter. Of course neither of those items were on the menu. However, there was a full selection of doughnuts. There were glazed, chocolate, jelly-filled,

Attitude Adjustment

and plain. There were no bagels, no toast, just fat-filled, sugar-loaded doughnuts. As a child, a breakfast of sugar would have been appealing to me. But as an adult, I don't even put sugar in my coffee. I began to get somewhat concerned that today wasn't going to be much better than yesterday. I took an orange juice, which was frozen solid, and returned to my room. Fortunately, we each had stashed a banana for a late night snack. I ate my orange juice and banana and thought about lunch.

Immediately following the so-called breakfast, the conference was underway. Patterned after a church service, the conference opened with a time of praise and worship. Two talented young women led in music and song. Their harmony blended beautifully with the soothing tones of the piano. The melodic sounds of feminine voices rang out as the rest of the women joined in singing.

The room was filled to capacity with women worshiping the risen Savior. Within minutes, tears began to fall freely down faces of young and not so young alike. They weren't singing as a form of entertainment. Nor were they merely saying words as they prayed. They were pressing in, reaching out, crying and waiting for a divine touch. These women were not merely asking for something spiritual, they were actually expecting it to happen.

Women all around me stood with their hands in the air praising the Lord. The colorful array of skin

Walking, Talking, Debating and Arguing with God

tones represented a wonderful diversity of race. Each pair of hands told the story of the woman at the other end of the arm. Soft smooth hands enhanced by manicured nails reached heavenward. Alongside were working hands, rough and callused with ragged, chipped nails.

Some fingers were dressed in diamonds and jewels while others were as natural as the day of their birth. Beautiful hands of youth adorned plump tender skin. Paper-thin, translucent skin stretched over aged fingers scarred and bent from the battles of time. Some of these were hands of mothers. Some were hands of sisters and grandmothers. All of these were the hands of daughters.

The Bible tells us God abides in the praises of His people. The truth of that Scripture was evident as a divine anointing spilled into the room. Heaven opened its doors and God descended to earth right in the middle of the Smokey Mountains. Although I couldn't see Him, I knew He was walking through the aisles. He was answering prayers and ministering to individuals as He passed. What I could see were the results of our heavenly visitor's afternoon stroll. His glory completely transformed women all around me. Expressions changed from desperate and longing to restful and fulfilled. Tears continued to flow, only now they were accompanied with smiles.

At some point, the music and singing had hushed. An indescribable calm blanketed the room. The Holy Spirit was showering women with precious gifts. Some

Attitude Adjustment

had their heads tilted back as "rain drops" of blessings sprinkled on their faces. Others knelt in total, complete, peaceful submission. I watched as women of all ages became as children resting safely in the strong arms of their loving Father.

These women were experiencing divine intervention. Many possessed a familiar glow that could only be the manifestation of the Almighty. I've experienced His holy presence so intensely that my natural body has literally collapsed under the supernatural weight. However, today I seemed to be the only one in the room not sharing this wonderful phenomenon.

First, I tried to blame my indifference on the praise and worship service. Having never heard any of the songs before, I was at a disadvantage. Everyone else was clapping and singing, having a good ol' time. Next, I tried to fool myself into believing nothing was wrong. Just because I didn't feel like singing and dancing around didn't mean I wasn't spiritual. Maybe I wanted to worship in a more reverent manner. I tried to convince myself that once the music and singing was over, I'd be able to enter into a reserved type of worship. In reality, I found the lingering quiet to be uncomfortably loud.

Perhaps it was the sound of a falling teardrop splashing to its fate that eventually broke the spiritual serenity. Whatever brought the awkward soundless situation to an end brought relief for me. I imagined this must be how it would feel to be invited to a party and end up at the wrong address by mistake. I was happy for these women. It was great that they were receiving a blessing. But at the same time I felt cheated. In frustration I silently screamed *God, what about me? Why am I being left out? After all, I'm Pentecostal. I've been saved, sanctified, and filled with the Holy Ghost.* I wanted to go home to my church. At least there I know the words to the songs.

As I thought about my church, the words of my pastor came to mind. Pastor Joe once said worship is like everything else. You get out of it what you put into it. That memory inspired me to pray. I asked forgiveness for being so cold and hard-hearted. I really did want to leave different than I came. In order to benefit from this conference, I would need a major attitude adjustment. The Lord was freely handing out gifts and I wanted one. The choice was mine. I could either open my heart to accept one of these holy gifts or deny myself a blessing.

The guest speaker was a slender, well-dressed black woman. She was poised but sassy, possessing a charming blend of heavenly refinement and earthly spunk. Her charisma was captivating, her prophetic gift intriguing. She spoke on being a new creature in Christ, using the metamorphosis of a butterfly to illustrate the change that takes place when Christ is allowed to encompass one's being.

Never had I heard the Word of God shared with such soulful enthusiasm. She served up Scripture with

Attitude Adjustment

more "spice" and "sauce" than any white woman would dare. Before long, my less than spiritual attitude went through a metamorphosis not unlike the butterfly in her story. Experiencing God's word proclaimed in such a carefree way caught me off guard. With my defenses down, my cold, hard heart began to warm and soften. The agony of my toothache was forgotten. It no longer mattered that I had never heard any of the songs that were sung. The need to go home to experience God subsided. As it turned out, I was at the correct address for the party after all.

God knew the needs of each woman in that room even before they arrived at the conference. He chose to honor us by fulfilling many of our specific desires. It was in His power to assign this duty to an angel as He often did in ancient days. Instead, He picked one of His human saints for the job. Personally, I'm glad He chose the latter. An actual heavenly being materializing in our midst would be too much to handle. Besides, it would have been a wasted trip. We'd be too frightened to hear the message.

I can't imagine this divine chore being executed any more gracefully. Not even by an angel. She fluttered from person to person like a butterfly delicately visiting every flower in the garden. Women were on the edge of their seats anticipating the privilege of having this black butterfly briefly light on their shoulder.

Our guest speaker became a liaison between the natural and supernatural worlds. Her metamorphosis story was periodically subject to what I call a Holy Ghost interruption. Sometimes right in the middle of a sentence she'd become silent, pausing as if trying to hear a whisper. Apparently she was listening to a still, quiet voice of which none of us was aware.

Taking the hand of the chosen audience member, she repeated aloud what had been silently spoken into her ear. Putting the story aside momentarily, she spoke directly and personally to the awestruck listener. Each time after delivering a divine message to a specific individual, she continued with her butterfly story. Surprisingly, she never lost her train of thought despite the frequent interruptions.

There was a different message for each person with whom she spoke. Sometimes she discussed a past situation in the person's life. Other times she told of something that would come to pass in the future. She told things of which she had no previous knowledge. Advice and encouragement were warmly and freely given. On occasion she would give answers to unspoken questions. Judging by the reaction of the women, she must have given the hoped for answers. Many times she didn't even understand the meaning of the messages she relayed. However, the meaning was never lost on the recipient.

The service did not end with the conclusion of the butterfly story. Our saintly messenger continued to walk around the room in an attitude of prayer. It was well past noon, but she didn't seem to be in a hurry to

Attitude Adjustment

leave. Oblivious to the lateness of the hour, she shared the secrets that supernaturally flooded her subconscious. Eventually the last divinely inspired message was delivered. Even then, she shared her time with all that requested a moment.

As I sat watching her, a strange sensation came over me. I felt as if we were in a barren desert with the heat beating down on us, our throats parched from thirst. Among us walked a woman with crystal clear, ice cold water, which she shared unselfishly. The water she shared was the Living Water of which Jesus Christ spoke. He promised that anyone who drinks of this Living Water will never thirst again. I had a revelation that day. Not only is this Living Water the ultimate thirst quencher, it's a pretty good attitude adjuster as well.

From the Mouth of Babes

As children, Bobby and Glenn argued with one another as most brothers do. During one such incident, Bobby's teasing prompted a swear word to fly from Glenn's lips. Bobby, feeling like the champion, continued his verbal torment. "See, Glenn, you cussed! And you call yourself a Christian. Christians don't cuss."
Frustrated, Glenn yelled, "Well, you call yourself a Christian. Christians don't make Christians cuss!"

Chapter Five

Butterfly

May 1, 1999

Whenever I read about the children of Israel being delivered out of Egypt, I'm amazed at how quickly they turned against God. They saw the Red Sea part, allowing them to cross over on dry land. The bottoms of their feet weren't even muddy when they reached the other side. Day and night they lived with the visible, tangible presence of God. Every day He was in front of their eyes in the form of a cloud. And every night they watched as He changed into a flaming fire lighting the way. Inconceivably, while living in the midst of such undeniable miracles, they lost their faith so easily. When Moses went to the mountaintop and didn't return as quickly as they preferred, they turned their backs on God. They built a fire and voluntarily gave up their jewelry and gold to be melted down and formed into the shape of a calf. Most unbelievable of all, they then bowed down in worship to the sculpture they'd made with their own hands.

Unfortunately, human nature hasn't changed much since that time. Lately my actions closely resembled those of the children of Israel. I had the chance to spend an entire weekend bathing in God's presence and eating from His Word. Yet instead of rejoicing, as one would expect of a Christian, I was miserable. I didn't want to come to this retreat, and had done everything in my power to have a terrible time.

I grumbled about the trip, the food, and the praise and worship service. The fact that I was suffering with a toothache added to my misery. Eventually, I softened as God's Word soaked through my crusty outer shell. I was refreshed, renewed, a changed person from only hours earlier. But as soon as I didn't get my way, I went right back to my doom-and-gloom state of mind.

At the conclusion of the morning service, three different workshops were scheduled. Our gifted guest speaker was teaching one called "A Closer Walk with Jesus." That was the class I wanted to attend. Her butterfly story and prophetic gift displayed in the morning service had left me desiring more. Plus, the temper tantrum I'd thrown all weekend was a good indication I needed a closer walk with Jesus.

Immediately after service, Bambi, Mom and I hurried out of the room to sign up for the workshop. It was already full when we reached the registration table. The only class with any openings remaining was a praise dance workshop. None of us was interested in praise dancing, but didn't have a whole lot of choice. As I recall, I referred to it as "a stupid dance class."

I remembered some of the ladies at my church back home had expressed a desire to start a dance ministry. Trying to make the most of a not so good situation, the least I could do was take notes to give to someone who would be interested. Who knows, maybe they'd get some hints on how to start such a ministry.

Only after class started did we learn it was going to be a hands-on learning experience. Everyone was encouraged to join in, try the moves, and learn a selected dance. All the ladies were excited about learning praise dance, with only three exceptions—Mom, Bambi, and me. Mom is far too self-conscious to dance around the house in front of her own children. There was no way she was going to join in this activity. Bambi was simply not interested. Dancing just wasn't her thing. I had my own reasons for not wanting to dance (mainly because I'd discarded my adjusted attitude when I couldn't attend the workshop of my choice). That was reason enough to be a grouch.

Walking, Talking, Debating and Arguing with God

The three of us sat in the back of the room, me with a pencil and paper taking notes. I didn't pay much attention to the dance steps or moves. My main focus was on the clothing worn by the dance instructors. They were dressed in layers of fabric. Their skirts were long and flowing, with matching pants underneath. This enabled them to spin and turn without compromising their modesty. Their long tops draped over their skirts prevented their hips from being too noticeable. This design provided total freedom of movement. Emphasizing that praise dancing is a type of worship, the women were careful to avoid any semblance of sexual content. Their goal was to worship and praise the Heavenly Father decently and in order.

The workshops were the last scheduled event until six o' clock that evening. Bambi, Mom, and I spent the afternoon driving around the Smokey Mountains and got lost for the second time that weekend. Just as before, we were last to arrive for the service. The room was set up with a dinner buffet against the back wall. The only empty table was so far in the back of the room my chair touched the buffet table when I was seated.

After dinner, our charismatic speaker effortlessly won the attention of the congregation. She said the service was going to be one of healing. Upon her request, women who needed physical healing stood to their feet. Next she asked everyone who had a financial need to rise. A few women answered the call by slowly

Butterfly

sliding out of their seats. Finally she said she knew there were women in the room who were dealing with chronic fear. Without further coaxing a couple women joined those already standing. In response to her gentle beckoning, women all across the room were patiently waiting for this servant of the Lord to approach them. Their eyes flashed with excitement as they imagined what heavenly message she'd share.

Approximately half of the women in the room were no longer seated, but quietly standing beside their chairs. I'm blessed that none of these areas of need related to me. I was also greatly relieved. None of my issues had been addressed. I didn't want to get that involved in the meeting. I wanted to sit in my chair propped against the buffet table and observe. I was more than satisfied to witness the healing hand of God deliver these women from various strongholds. I hadn't raised my hand, and wasn't asked to stand. And to insure my role as spectator, I avoided any eye contact with the speaker as she lightly moved about like a butterfly on a gentle breeze.

She wove gracefully around tables and in between chairs. Every few steps she'd focus on someone standing for prayer. Moving toward them she began to speak words of prophecy. Some of the women squealed like teenagers as she revealed their specific need. It was if someone was whispering into her ear details concerning each woman's life. Not only did she speak of the problem, but offered the solution as well.

Walking, Talking, Debating and Arguing with God

She was reading these women's life stories. The difference being, she had read ahead a few chapters, and was sharing some of the upcoming events.

Making her way to the front of the room, she stood with her back to the congregation momentarily. Slowly, precisely, she turned to face her captive audience. Without a word, she began to move deliberately through the maze of tables, chairs, and women. A chill tingled through me causing a spontaneous shiver. A too-familiar sick feeling settled in my stomach. I knew she was coming for me. Hoping to discourage her, I quickly shifted my gaze. Undeterred, she continued to advance in my direction.

Along her path, women reached out to touch her. They were thinking she would stop next to them. I knew better. She was on her way to the very last table at the very back of the room. I was becoming somewhat agitated, trying to make sense of her actions. With so many women wanting her attention, why would she pick on me. I was just minding my own business, using extreme caution not to draw her attention. There were several tables between her and me, yet with every step she drew closer. I just wanted her to stop. I felt an incredible urge to flee. Inside I became that same shy little girl I had been in school. If only I could hide out in the restroom until she forgot about me.

This ebony butterfly had a meadow of flowers on which to light. Each blossom displayed their pretty

Butterfly

petals in hopes of luring the desirable creature. Dancing on air the black beauty fluttered past all the lovely flowers. At the very back of the meadow was a prickly, uninviting thistle. That was where the delicate creature ever so softly touched down and lowered her wings.

Feeling her hand warm on my shoulder, my body stiffened. Looking straight ahead, I tried to convey she'd made a mistake. Hopefully, she'd decide an unbending, sticker-covered thistle was not the most comfortable place to rest. However, this butterfly's charm was second only to her wisdom. She knew how to deal with thistles.

Taking me by the hand, she tenderly pulled me from my chair. As much as I wanted to remain rooted, my legs deserted me. Against the wishes of the rest of me, they lifted my body. There'd be no escaping now. I was standing eye to eye with the human butterfly. Her face was pleasant and unassuming, seemingly unaware of my negative attitude. A closer look into her eyes told me there was little about me of which she was unaware.

Knocking down all my defenses, she asked if she could pray for me. What was I supposed to say? "No thank you, I don't need prayer." If anyone in that room needed prayer, I did. The compassion with which she posed her question dissolved my fear. No longer feeling threatened, my spirit surrendered, enabling me to enter into an attitude of prayer. After a brief prayer

Walking, Talking, Debating and Arguing with God

requesting God's blessings in my life, she said "Amen." I smiled, thanked her and started to sit down.

She didn't release my hand, or her gaze into my eyes. She wasn't staring at me, but through me, looking deep into my soul. What could she possibly be seeing? Although curious, I wasn't about to ask. Instead I was going to fight her! I prepared myself for a mental battle, determined not to feed her any information to use against me. If she were truly a prophet of God, she wouldn't need any help from me.

As her focus changed back to me, she inquired, "You've been praying for something for a long time and haven't received an answer yet. Right?" I was less than impressed with that question. Was that the best she could do? What were the chances she'd get that one wrong? Of course I have unanswered prayers. Doesn't everybody? The instant she said that to me, I thought of one particular prayer, but I didn't share it with her. She didn't know me, and I didn't see the need to tell her my personal business. I nodded in silent agreement.

Not waiting for my response, she proceeded to explain why this particular prayer hadn't been answered. With the sweetest smile and most motherly tone she said, "You haven't received the answer to this particular prayer because you're holding your gifts from God." Well, I wasn't sure where she was getting her information, but she was way off base with that one. I was starting to have serious doubts about her gift of prophecy. A prophet hears directly from our all-knowing Creator. If God places something in the heart of a prophet to share, it will be truth. God is truth. He wouldn't give an incorrect message to be relayed.

Her statement made me all the more ready for battle. She was just wrong. No longer intimidated by her confidence, I stared back into her dark eyes. I began to mentally list all the things I did for the ministry. Whenever we have a car wash or garage sale to raise money, I participate. On Thanksgiving when we deliver food to the needy in our community, I'm one of the few who actually go door to door and do the work. It was I who planned, coordinated, and participated in singing Christmas carols at the doorsteps of the government housing residents in our neighborhood. And I don't even sing well. (Most of the residents are elderly. They'd cry as we stood in their threshold singing. I always said it was because we were so off key.) I always give to special offerings, collections, and building funds. When we needed classrooms built, I wore a nail apron and hung Sheetrock. All our church events I take pictures, with which I started and maintain a church scrapbook. All the film and photo albums are paid for and donated by me. Along the same lines, I tape special events and services, using my own video equipment and supplies. In order to decorate our bare walls, I purchased satin and trim and made banners. The table runner on the communion table was made and donated by me. I started the

Walking, Talking, Debating and Arguing with God

children's ministry and have been teaching class every Wednesday night since. Many of the children wouldn't be in church on Wednesdays if I didn't pick them up and take them home each week. During summer months I take the children of the church on field trips. Many times I'm the only adult on these outings. I've opened my home to the entire congregation on more than one occasion for picnics and fellowship. I even do all the alterations on the pastor's suits and his family's clothing for no charge. Who was she to tell me I was holding my gifts from God? Boy did it feel good to pat myself on the back. What kind of comeback would Madame Butterfly have now?

The oddest thing was happening while these thoughts were racing through my brain. As I mentally spoke, she nodded her head in acknowledgment. Her sweet expression never changed. Her eyes twinkled, and she wore the most understanding smile. She was displaying good listening skills, but what was she listening to? She couldn't have heard anything I'd said, because I hadn't opened my mouth. I was saying these things in my mind. When I'd finished, she softly said, "I know, I know, Butterfly. But God wants more." That response left me confused on two fronts. First of all, why was she saying "I know"? What did she know? How could she know? Second of all, how could God possibly want more? More what? I didn't have more.

She said, "I see you dancing." I thought, *If you do, it's a long time ago.* And it's not in church. It's in nightclubs

Butterfly

before I was saved, and the dance moves aren't exactly holy. At that moment, I saw myself in one of my favorite outfits I wore in the 70s, my white hip-hugger pants and mauve crushed-velvet halter top. It was embarrassing to think this spiritual lady might "see" me in such attire and atmosphere. That uncomfortable memory vanished when she said, "I see you dancing before the Lord."

There she went, confusing me again. About the time I was convinced she must have had some sort of divine communication channel, she'd say something that just didn't relate to me whatsoever. With absolute conviction, and authority she told me, "You're a dancer. A praise dancer." With less confidence than previously, I assumed my mental battle position. No I'm not, I thought. You've got the wrong girl. This time her verbal response to my mental rebuttal was so direct it frightened me. Putting her hand on her hip and using her soulful black culture, she said, "Oh no I don't have the wrong girl, Girlfriend. The Lord says you're a praise dancer. You know when you're at church and the music is jamming. You know that feeling you get, like you just can't keep still. You know how deep down in the depths of your soul you wanna get out of your seat and move. Why do you think you feel that way? Who do you think filled your body with rhythm? God put that dance in your step! He gave you that gift and you're holding it from Him."

She got my attention that time. She'd never been to my church to see me during praise and worship. It's for certain the attitude I'd carried around this weekend was no indication that I wanted to do anything other than go home. Yet she had just described me better than I could have done myself. She not only knew my thoughts but my most suppressed feelings as well. All of a sudden, I was interested in what she had to say, and was mentally waving a white flag. The battle was over.

Continuing, she asked if I'd attended the praise dance workshop. I suspected she knew the answer. Nevertheless, I wanted to answer this question. For the first time since she'd prayed for me, I was going to offer a verbal response. So when she said, "Did you attend the praise dance workshop?" I simply said, "Yes." That was a truthful answer. I did attend the workshop. No longer had the last syllable rolled from my tongue than I heard familiar voices calling out. It was my very own cheering section, Mom and Bambi. I couldn't believe what they were saying. "Yea, but she didn't dance," Mom said. "That's right," Bambi agreed, "she didn't dance." Laughing, I sarcastically said, "Thanks a lot. Traitors."

Turning to face the speaker, my cheeks flushed with guilt. I'd been caught with my hand in the cookie jar. Faking disbelief, in a voice slightly higher than before, she said, "What? You didn't dance? Why did you go to the praise dance workshop if you weren't going to dance?" Before I could answer, those two familiar voices piped up again. "The other classes were full," Bambi explained. "She didn't want to go to that

Butterfly

class," Mom added. "Tell her what you said about it." Obviously Mom and Bambi were thoroughly enjoying watching me squirm. "What did you say about it?" asked the speaker, not letting that golden opportunity slip past. Dropping my head like a shameful child, I muttered under my breath, "I said I don't want to go to a stupid praise dance workshop." "What kind of workshop did you say?" she asked, forcing me to repeat myself. "A stupid praise dance workshop."

Mom and Bambi weren't the only ones having fun. The speaker was definitely a class act, but was losing her struggle to disguise a smile. "If you didn't dance what did you do?" As ridiculous as it sounded, I told her I was taking notes. "If you aren't a praise dancer, why were you taking notes in a praise dance workshop?" "I was taking them for some ladies in my church who want to start a dance ministry." She closed her eyes and shook her head back and forth with sass. "Butterfly, you weren't taking notes for those other women. You just thought you were. Baby, those notes were for you. Because you're a praise dancer."

Taking a handful of my hair and showing it to me, she said, "Why do you think God hasn't let you cut your hair?" It had never occurred to me that God paid any attention to my hairstyle. By this time, tears were dripping off my face onto the floor, as the Holy Spirit had finally penetrated my untrusting, doubting, cynical façade. Between sobs I answered, "Because it's naturally curly. When it's short it gets frizzy and looks awful."

Walking, Talking, Debating and Arguing with God

With her fingers under my chin she tilted my face up to meet hers. Her voice had a lower, serious tone as she spoke these words; "Your hair is your glory. God didn't let you grow your hair that long for no reason. Your hair is anointed just like Samson's. But you know that already. Don't you? You've been told that before. I'm not the first to tell you your hair is anointed."

She was right! I had forgotten about the first time those words were prophesied over me. It had been in a church of a different denomination, in a different town. At the time, the prophecy sounded so bizarre I wrote it down in a notebook. Later when referring to those notes, I found that the first prophecy was almost exactly one year prior. It happened in April of 1998.

Gently stroking my hair she continued, "Your hair is a blessing. You will dance before the Lord. I see you dancing before the Lord. This is a gift God has given you. Just like the gift of your hair. As you dance before the Lord strongholds will come down." Pausing for a brief moment, she held my hand and squeezed to emphasize her next statement. Her eyes narrowed with intensity. "Your loved ones will come into the kingdom of God. Those in your family." Upon hearing her speak of my family I thought of my siblings who didn't know Christ as their Savior. She nodded as if she were looking at them with me. Stressing the word *your*, she repeated, "In *your* family." This time the images of my grown daughters became visible to me. Again she nodded in agreement as if saying yes, them too. Amazingly,

Butterfly

she said it one last time, "In *your* family." My body trembled as a new image began to form in my mind. I was almost too afraid to allow it to manifest itself, frightened of the outcome. Then as clear as if he were standing next to me, I saw the smiling eyes of my dear husband. It is for him that I pray unceasingly.

Tenderly removing my fear, she said, "Yes. They're coming in. God has promised you answers to your prayers. He's going to do it. Not when you think He needs to. He doesn't do it as quickly as you want, but He is faithful. Just stand on the things He has said to you. Stand. Just stand. And dance. Dance before the Lord. You can do all things through Christ who strengthens you."

Trying to comprehend all that had transpired left me mentally and physically drained. My composure was that of a wet noodle. Before I was seated, all the praise dancers from the church came and encircled me, praying down glory from heaven. A young lady knelt at my feet and prayed for God to bless their steps. I was humbled by such an act of humility. They had all finished praying and were gathered around me when someone made an observation. We all had butterflies in our hair. Without any planning, the praise dancers and myself each had worn some type of butterfly decoration in our hair. Mine was the craft item I had painted on the first night of the retreat. It was actually a pin, designed to be worn on clothing. As I was leaving my hotel room to go to service, I stuck it in my hair. I'd planned on giving it to my granddaughter upon returning home, but I guess I'll keep it. Oh yeah, I guess I'd better dance too.

Dorothy Lee Prophecy, April 1998

"Little shy child with the golden halo. You with this beautiful hair, God has blessed you with this hair. It is your glory. I believe God uses the anointing He has placed on your hair. You are shy and quiet, but God is going to bring you out of that. You are a willing vessel. You are tenderhearted and sensitive and loving. You do not know the power of your words. Your words have power. Speak forth and watch them work. God has not forgotten you. You have not been left out. God says to you, listen to your dreams at night, for it is I who gives you those dreams. Don't look to the past. Don't look back. Time is short. In the days ahead, you will need to draw closer to me. Don't be discouraged, everything will be all right. Just draw nearer to me, my precious child. Things are going to get better. They will get worse first, but they will get better. Pray for the rest of your family for I love them too. Stand in the gap for them."

Dorothy Lee had another woman sing a prophecy over me. She sang in tongues. Then she interpreted the message in tongues as:

"You have the gift of a heavenly song. Sing this song. Sing it at night when you are alone with me to encourage yourself. You will sing in the Hosanna choir. You will sing in the Hosanna choir."

Butterfly

From the Mouth of Babes

Teacher: "Remember to build your house upon the Lord Jesus Christ."

Jimi: "That would squish Him!"

Chapter Six

Promises, Bargains, and Covenants

September 20, 1999

Human nature often causes us to believe we can bargain with our Creator. Most of us have offered to make a deal with God at least once. Sometimes we act as if the Almighty is nothing more than a magic genie. I wonder how many times He's heard statements like, "Dear God, if you will grant this wish, I promise to be good." That seems to be a popular prayer when we've gotten ourselves into a less than desirable situation. Promises come easy when we need God to deliver us from messes of own making. Too

Walking, Talking, Debating and Arguing with God

often, after God has answered our prayer, we find it difficult, if not impossible, to hold up our end of the bargain.

Recently God confronted me about this very scenario. For years I've prayed that my husband would accept the Lord as his personal savior. Gary is a genuinely good man. He just doesn't acknowledge Jesus Christ as the one and only way to heaven. God has blessed Gary with desirable characteristics that many Bible-reading, church-attending, born-again Christians lack. The first thing I noticed about him when we met was the way he put those around him at ease. When engaged in conversation, he looks you in the eye and is an interested listener. These listening skills are evident with corporate executives and young children alike.

Coworkers and subordinates appreciate the calming effect Gary has in the hectic business environment. His wisdom and compassionate ear have attracted men and women to him for counsel on a variety of issues. The respect and dignity with which he treats everyone has found him favor with people of all lifestyles, religious beliefs, and political preferences.

A number of female friends and family members have expressed that I have the ideal husband. I don't have to balance the checkbook or pay the bills. Gary's self-discipline and organizational skill allows us to live comfortably within our budget while continually preparing for our financial future. Gary is the cook in our house. He can prepare a delicious meal while I'm staring hopelessly into the refrigerator trying to decide on a menu. Most nights he cooks dinner and I clean the dishes and kitchen. Another chore the two of us share is laundry duty. He doesn't like to fold clothes, so he loads and empties the washer and dryer and I fold and put away.

One of his hobbies is gardening so he keeps our yard looking nice. He stays so busy working around the house and yard I seldom have a "honey do" list for him. He's learned the secret of how to live peacefully with a woman. By taking an active part in the mundane chores of marriage, he's able to relax and enjoy a ball game on TV without the sound of a nagging wife ringing in his ears.

When Gary married me, he virtually married my whole family. I'm the oldest sibling of six girls and two boys. Gary has voluntarily worked on cars, houses, lawnmowers, and fences for my single sisters. He's spent weekends working in the gardens of others while his own is in desperate need of attention. Seldom does an evening go by without a phone call seeking his assistance with computer related problems. His home office has computers sitting on shelves, desks, and on the floor all waiting for him to "do a little work on them." The only payment Gary has ever accepted for his work is a "thank-you."

Six of my siblings have gone to college. With one exception, Gary and I have helped each of them as they

Walking, Talking, Debating and Arguing with God

struggled with juggling work and school. In every circumstance he cheerfully offered financial assistance regardless of the risk. People approach Gary for help because their dignity and self-respect is not jeopardized. They know their secrets, whether financial or personal, are safe with him.

If you have Gary as a friend, you have a treasure. His honesty, although at times painful, is surprisingly refreshing. He shares his thoughts sparingly, but every word is sincere. He's genuine, yet complicated, not fitting into any mold. Just about the time you think you've got him figured out, he'll express an opinion that'll blow all your preconceived ideas of him.

His conservative appearance is in direct contrast to his fun-filled, ornery, playful side. I teasingly accuse him of dual personalities. On one hand he's highly intelligent, technically trained, and has a passion for electronics. On the other hand, he's creative, artistic, and a nonconformist. Monday through Friday he's a supervisor in the business world. On weekends, when he's not gardening or landscaping, he's chopping firewood. His hands, scratched and bruised from building our stone patio and fireplace in the fall, will plant the delicate flowers in the spring.

Gary is an understanding father, a loving grandfather, and a sensitive, devoted husband. He's my soul mate for whom I thank God every day. Also daily I ask the Holy Spirit to dwell in him. Countless times I've promised to do anything God asked if Gary would

Promises, Bargains, and Covenants

become a born again believer. I'd give my life for him if I knew he'd be guaranteed a heavenly eternity.

I'm not the first wife to pray this desperate prayer. God heard my cries and decided to test my faith concerning the matter. Admittedly I'm glad He didn't take my suggestion asking me to make the ultimate sacrifice. He explained that because of Calvary, that price had already been paid.

In biblical times God required rather extreme measures from some of His children. Some were asked to leave their families to go to undisclosed destinations. One servant was required to remain naked day and night for two years. What He asked of me was far less dramatic. He asked me to dance. He said if I'd dance in worship before Him, He'd usher my husband into His Holy Kingdom.

Dancing had been an important part of my life before I allowed Jesus in. I coined the phrase "I live to dance." Dancing was not merely a form of exercise. Had it been, I would have worn jogging pants, sweatshirts, and no makeup when I went out. For me, as with most young girls, dancing was a tool by which I gained the attention I craved. I knew in my tight pants and halter tops, and with a few well-rehearsed moves, I could capture the eye of every person in the room.

Men would send drinks to my table and buy me dinner. Although I never accepted their offers to drive me home, or their many other colorful offers, I was nevertheless sinning. By knowingly contributing to the

Walking, Talking, Debating and Arguing with God

lustful nature of man, I not only caused them to sin, but was guilty of the same. When I became a Christian, I became a new creature. The Bible says old things will pass away, all things will become new. Dancing was part of my old nature that I happily left behind.

Of all the requests God could have required I just couldn't understand why He chose dancing. When I was a child being raised in Pentecostal churches, everything was a "sin." Makeup, earrings, long pants were all taboo. Television, movies, cards and most other forms of entertainment were considered ungodly.

As an adult I attended a Pentecostal church where a couple of church members wanted to start a dance ministry. I wasn't entirely sure what they had in mind. But I didn't really give the idea much thought, because I had no intention of having any part of it. The image of someone dancing in church was almost impossible for my mind to comprehend. It was completely opposite of what I perceived as being righteous.

A few months later, I attended a women's retreat in Knoxville, where God called me to dance. That was the first time I'd ever seen a praise dance. I was struggling to become accustomed to watching someone dance in church, and God was asking me to participate! At the time, I felt compelled to obey because of the directness of His message. Once I got home three hours later, my willingness was replaced with doubt and fear.

Dancing may sound rather minor, but it felt major. As a matter of fact, it made me angry. For God to

Promises, Bargains, and Covenants

expect me to dance in front of a room full of people seemed like punishment. What did I do to deserve such treatment? I'd been attending church regularly, reading my Bible and praying every day. I'd been attentive to God's voice and trying to live according to His word. Had I overlooked something? Had I unintentionally broken some biblical law for which I had to pay retribution?

As if my memory were a VCR, I kept rewinding and playing the "tape" over and over. Each time the message was the same. It sounded so easy. I want my husband to become a Christian, and in order for that to happen, I have to dance. Of course no one can be danced into heaven. This was about obedience, not dancing.

The burden I carried for my husband's eternal soul became priority. There was nothing I wouldn't do if he'd accept the most precious gift of all. I'd die for him if necessary. As it turned out, death would have to occur. To live in God's perfect will, my "flesh" would have to die.

Throughout God's Word, His promises are twofold. He says He'll do a particular thing for us if we do a particular thing for Him. The Bible tells us God is incapable of a lie. So when He said my husband would enter into the Kingdom if I danced, I believed Him.

What choice did I have? What else could I do? I'll tell you what I did. I went and sought counsel from Monica. Not only is she my friend, but being a pastor, I thought she might be able to help me find a loophole allowing me an escape. I met with her the next day during her lunch break to discuss my problem. She listened intently and empathized as I ranted and raved for nearly an hour about how unfairly God was treating me. She offered me a glass of water in an attempt to calm me. My mouth was dry and my body shaking from frustration. After I'd finished venting, she softly replied, "Well, Robin, you know you have to do it." The twinkle in her eyes revealed the enthusiasm she had failed to conceal. I knew in my heart she was right. Of course I had to, but I didn't have to like it.

Our small country church had only recently started singing songs other than hymns sung by my grandmother a child. It isn't exactly a contemporary, progressive congregation. What would the traditional, country-music-loving saints think about this? I couldn't bear to imagine their horror. Apparently Monica had more faith in their open-mindedness. In her sweet, gentle voice, she said, "Oh Robin, isn't is wonderful? You're a praise dancer!" I thought, *Yeah it's easy for you to be excited. You're not the one that has to get up in front of the church and dance.*

Relying on her strong leadership skills, Monica asked, "So when would you like to start? How about Mother's Day?" She couldn't be serious. Mother's Day was the following weekend. I'd only seen one praise dance ever, and didn't pay much attention to it. I didn't have any music, I didn't know any dances, and I certainly didn't have anything appropriate to wear.

Promises, Bargains, and Covenants

Immediately I began to explain why it would be absolutely impossible for me to pull off something like this in less than a week. Naturally, my words went in one of Monica's ears and out the other. Smiling she said, "Robin, God has called you to do this. He'll enable you to do what He's asked of you. I have CDs you can borrow, so you have music. You're a seamstress, can you make an outfit in time?" I didn't get the chance to answer before she said, "The whole service is going to be led by women. We've been trying to find a woman to do some kind of "special." Your dance will be the "special." You're both a woman and a mother. It'll be perfect!" The two of us engaged in conversation, one bubbling over with joy, the other steaming with anger, must have been a comical sight.

Over the following week I designed and created an outfit. I borrowed a CD containing the song I'd heard at the retreat. I went into my sewing room, closed the door and played the CD. As the song played, I stood in front of my full-length mirror and prayed, reminding God how this was not my idea but His. If He wanted me to dance, He was going to have to teach me how. His grace enabled me to remember most of the dance. The other steps He showed me as I went. After one divine dance lesson I could execute the moves. Now I had a few days of practice to polish the rough spots so they'd flow as intended.

I invited Mom and Dad to watch my final practice on the day before my debut. Being slightly apprehensive about dancing in front of Gary, I didn't mention it to him. Besides, he was busy working in the garden. My audience of two situated themselves on the sofa while I fumbled with the CD. Seconds away from my first performance I stepped up to "center stage." During the song's instrumental intro before my first movement, Gary walked into the house. He sat down in one of our wingback chairs and watched as I danced around our living room. At the conclusion of my dress rehearsal he slowly clapped his hands and whispered, "Wow."

Mother's Day came faster than ever that year. Before church started, those who were participating in leading service met in Pastor's office for prayer. We stood in a circle and held hands as Pastor asked for God's anointing to cover each of us. Never do I remember experiencing such anxiety over a situation. I was incapable of controlling my tears or my wobbly legs. Like electricity, my body tremors ran out through my hands, continuing through to the hands of the person on either side of me, causing them to tremble as well. Our associate pastor happened to be one of the people who were now shaking in unison with me.

Before we went into the sanctuary he said, "Robin, God has not given you a spirit of fear, but of peace. You're stepping out in faith, doing as He's requested. He'll be with you, and comfort you, and give you the anointing you need. Don't worry about the people in the congregation. You aren't doing this for them.

Promises, Bargains, and Covenants

You're doing this for the Lord, and your obedience will be pleasing in His eyes."

The power of his words seeped into my being, providing strength to proceed to the front of the sanctuary. Waiting for the first note of music, I stood motionless in silent prayer. I wasn't asking for boldness, or even for help in remembering the moves. My prayer was that my praises be as fragrant incense when they drifted down the street of gold.

Within seconds my greatest fear was met head on. I was actually dancing in church! No longer was I concerned with the reaction and thoughts of the congregation. The overwhelming presence of the Lord caused me to feel as though I was no longer on earth, but somewhere sacred and holy. My body began to gently sway and move, as the faint sound of music encircled me. My soul was swimming in a sea of worship.

The surreal experience concluded in peaceful emotion. People all across the room were sharing this special moment. Hands and voices were lifted high as they magnified the King of Kings. The joyous sounds of God's people proclaiming their love for Him lingered long after my praise dance had ended.

On my way out of the sanctuary, our praise and worship leader approached me. Suppressing tears, all he said was "wow." I was intrigued that his reaction was the same as displayed by my husband earlier. This repeated response caused me to reflect on something one of the dancers at the women's retreat had shared.

Walking, Talking, Debating and Arguing with God

After congratulating me on my divinely appointed role, she told me this was a ministry that especially touched the hearts of men. Many had expressed how watching praise dancing enhanced their own personal worship. In general men seem to be motivated by visuals rather than emotions. Praise dancing creates a tangible form of worship that can be seen as well as felt.

Over the next three months our church sponsored two other events where they scheduled me to dance. I choreographed and performed a couple of dances with the youth group. Conquering the recent foreboding challenges caused a renewal of my spirit. Praise dancing was the biggest, most uncomfortable step I'd ever taken in my walk with the Lord. Initially the very idea was inconceivable. Now that the experience was history I could return to the traditional form of worship.

The date of my last praise dance was August 8. By the end of the month, I was experiencing the recurring feeling of being incomplete. You know the looming sensation that you're forgetting something, like maybe the stove was still on when you left the house. These feelings became more prevalent, increasing my misery as the weeks went by. Searching my heart for answers resulted in confusion. The source of my anxiety was the bargain I'd made with God, but what was the connection. My justification was, "God asked me to dance and I did what He asked. Why doesn't He leave me alone?"

Promises, Bargains, and Covenants

By September my brain had become preoccupied with the idea of praise dancing. This cranial obsession crept into my prayer life. My thoughts repeatedly fixated on the same familiar images, interrupting private conversations with my Savior. All hours of the day and night, my subconscious was filled with music and dancing. Physical movement and motion disturbed my slumber on numerous occasions.

One night I dreamed of several women wearing long, colorful, flowing dresses. Whirling and spinning in slow motion gave the effect of dancing on air. However, they weren't on a cloud, but in my church and I was one of them. I woke with a start, sat straight up in bed, breathless, my heart racing. This mustn't continue. I was suffering from sleep depravation, exhausted from dancing till dawn night after night.

My spiritual journey characterizes a hike rather than a walk. The Bible says the path we must take is straight and narrow. Sometimes the narrow path is straight up a mountain. I longed for my life to be as it was prior to my dancing dilemma. However, my journey had already advanced beyond that crossroad.

For years I'd asked the Holy Spirit to direct me toward some type of ministry where I could be used for His glory. It's just that dancing wasn't what I had in mind. It wasn't my place to question the Creator of the universe, but I wouldn't be the first or the last to do so. Our flawed human spirit makes it inevitable. Before I'd be willing to jump in with both feet, I wanted some answers. Like, why dancing? Why couldn't I do something else instead? Why couldn't obedience be easier?

My shy, timid nature has always been a stronghold in my life. Now it was hindering a supernatural plan for my future. I feared putting my desires above those of the Almighty, yet feared making the wrong decision. Also I feared people might accuse me of vying for the spotlight when in reality I preferred the safety of the shadows. This debilitating fear had blinded my spiritual eyes and paralyzed my dance. Insecurity caused me to question whether the constant tugging on my heart was indeed heaven sent. The origin of my cardiovascular trauma was soon to be revealed in a most unforgettable fashion.

On a cool crisp September evening, driving to church, I was enjoying some rare quiet time alone with my thoughts. My peaceful tranquility was jarred to the core when a firm, male voice shattered the silence, "You owe me this." My heart rate instantly and drastically increased to a dangerous pace. My chest tightened with pain, causing my breathing to stop momentarily. Crying aloud with terror, I gasped for air. The excessive deterioration of my nervous state prevented me from maintaining control of the car. Pulling over to the side of the road, my hands adhered to the steering wheel like glue. Fearing for my safety, I prepared to sacrifice my money and car.

Promises, Bargains, and Covenants

Collecting every ounce of strength, I shot a quick glance at the rearview mirror. Mentally braced to encounter a man's reflection, what I saw was the back seat of my car. Ever so slowly, I turned and looked over my shoulder. Unable to discover the man belonging to the voice, I leaned completely over and surveyed the floorboard behind the driver's seat. My back seat was empty. Terror changed to relief that was quickly exchanged for confusion. Dizzy from my emotional roller coaster ride I turned to face the front. My hands still pasted to the wheel, I sat and waited for my muscles to relax.

Becoming cognizant enough to pray, I recognized the still small voice of my Heavenly Father. The delivery of the message was softer, but the content unchanged. "You owe me this. Music, rhythm, dance, movement all come from me. They're gifts I've given to my people with which, they can worship, praise, and glorify me. I want my children to have life and have it more abundantly. These gifts were meant to encourage and uplift the spirits of my children. These sacred gifts were stolen and perverted by Satan.

"It is I who put dance in your step and rhythm in your body. Yet for years you used my gifts for the enemy. Your dance seduced and lured many deeper into Satan's lair. Now you must dance for me. I will anoint your steps making them a blessing, that I be glorified. Your dance will usher people into worship. As you dance in my presence many more souls will be won for my holy kingdom. I will take you from glory to glory."

After spending a little more time in prayer on the side of the road, I continued on my way. Upon arriving at church, I walked directly to Pastor's office. I shared with him my dreams and supernatural encounter with the great I Am. God was calling me into a ministry of dance and I needed to make sure it fit with Pastor's plan for our church. God's word was confirmed when Pastor told me of a vision he had shared with the congregation a couple weeks prior. I'd been teaching a children's class in another room so this was my first knowledge of Pastor's experience. I listened as he described our sanctuary filled with women dressed in white formal dresses. He said, "They were everywhere, dancing around the pews, up and down the aisle and at the altar. It was beautiful."

Pastor and I had received the same dream from the same Dream Maker. An important lesson was revealed to me through these recent circumstances. People make bargains. God makes covenants. He expects total commitment, not a token. It took me forty years to raise both of my hands in submission to the Holy Spirit. Now I must surrender the rest of my body. It defies human logic for God to call a grandmother twenty years past her prime and twenty pounds overweight to be a dancer, but He did. He spoke it and I've accepted it without further questions.

From the Mouth of Babes

From a class about the forty years in the wilderness:

Nannette: "Wow! You're forty years old. Were you there?"

Chapter Seven

COMMAND PERFORMANCE

October 29, 1999

Being an extremely shy child, I never learned to pray aloud in front of others. So, naturally, it remains difficult for me as an adult. The first time I had ever prayed in front of anyone, other than young children, was last year. Mary Linda, a Christian artist who visited my church, asked if I would join her and a friend, Jan, as prayer partners. We met at Mary Linda's house for dinner and prayer once a month. Conflicting schedules prevented our prayer group from lasting more than a few months. But its rich experience helped me to grow spiritually.

One day Mary Linda called to see if I would be interested in being a prayer partner for an upcoming Bible conference that would be held in our city. I agreed without any question.

Never having been involved with any type of conference before, I had no idea what to expect. In my mind I pictured Mary Linda, Jan, and myself sitting in the living room in our intimate prayer group of days gone by. I was excited about seeing them again, and sharing some of God's wonderful blessings in my life.

Well I was right about the prayer meeting being held at Mary Linda's house. However, that was the only thing I had right. On the first scheduled meeting, I arrived a few minutes early. Jan wasn't going to be able to make it, but a woman named Kendra was going to take her place. Mentally, I convinced myself that I was a grown-up and I could pray in front of Kendra whom I had just met. Besides, it was still a small, intimate group with just three of us.

Just as Mary Linda looked at her watch and decided we should start praying, there was a knock on the door. Someone else had come to join our group. I thought, *Oh no! Four people, I've never prayed in front of four people. It's okay, I told myself. We are all women. Certainly, I can pray in front of women.* The next knock on the door caused me great stress. A man entered the living room and joined our prayer group. He was followed by more knocks on the door. By this time the living room was packed and not only with women.

Command Performance

It never occurred to me that someone other than Mary Linda, Jan, and myself would be involved in this prayer group. As this first meeting started, the reality of my crippling shyness overwhelmed me. I tried to hide the expression of fear that must have taken over my face. Looking around the room at the crowd caused my stomach to literally become upset. How could I have agreed to do something that would make me so terribly uncomfortable? What was I thinking? I considered excusing myself and confessing nausea, but I was too scared to leave. This debilitating shyness with which I have battled my entire life had me paralyzed. I couldn't leave, and was afraid I'd be sick if I stayed.

Frantically, I tried to come up with some feasible course of action. While contemplating several scenarios, I heard Kendra suggest we sing some praise and worship songs. What a relief! If nothing else it would buy me more time to devise a plan of escape.

Mary Linda sat down at her baby grand piano and started playing "Amazing Grace." I doubt if a more anointed song has ever been written. Members of the prayer team softly sang along. Closing my eyes, I tuned out everything except the flowing, melodic sound of this impromptu choir. The words of this ancient hymn brought me comfort.

When the song ended, whispered praises could be heard throughout the room. Mary Linda prayed while her fingers gently caressed the keys of the lovely instrument. As we continued in worship, the sweet presence of the Lord tenderly fell on each of us. An unimaginable peace flowed through my spirit as it fell in sync with God.

One by one people in the room spoke from their hearts to their Heavenly Father. No longer was this a room of strangers. Somewhere between the praises and the intimate worship, we had become family. We may not have shared many earthly interests, but what we did share was far more inspiring. We shared a genuine desire for the presence of the Almighty. We shared the same Savior.

When it came my turn to pray, I was amazed by the ease with which my words came forth. The usual fears of speaking in front of a group never manifested. Every thought of fear had vanished. My only thoughts were on Jesus, as I stood in His awesome presence. At that moment, the privilege of speaking one on one with Him consumed my consciousness. I began to thank Him for allowing me to be a part of this prayer team. I gave Him praise for enabling me to be a small part of the glorious work being done for His kingdom.

I agreed to be a prayer partner for one reason, to be used for the glory of God. All I had to offer was my willingness. There wasn't much I could do in the Lord's army because of my timid nature. But, as a prayer warrior I could be a strong soldier. While praying and seeking His will, the Holy Spirit spoke to me. With all my feelings of insignificance, He promised to use me during the upcoming seminar.

Command Performance

God would have to make some major adjustments to my personality if He planned on using me. He had already worked a miracle in my life tonight by giving me the strength to pray. Not only had I managed to speak words, I had poured out my soul with total honesty. And I did so without collapsing from fear. If God was going to use me in any other fashion, He would have to perform yet another miracle.

Opening night of the seminar came at last. It was held at the prestigious Opryland Hotel. The thirty-minute drive from home to the seminar gave me ample time to become a nervous wreck. I kept playing the same scenes over and over again in my mind. First I had to park and walk through the giant doors opening onto a majestic stairway. Most certainly there would be guests lounging at the courtesy seating areas at the bottom of the stairs. This meant there would be plenty of eyes to watch as I (hopefully) gracefully descended the stairs. Of course the ballroom in which the seminar was held was at the end of a magnificent long hall. The hall naturally would be filled with people who had nothing better to do than watch as lone women uncomfortably made their way past. If I succeeded in reaching the end of the hall, there would be the trauma of walking into the Presidential Ballroom filled with people whom I've never met.

My hands were perspiring at the thought of this imagined medieval gauntlet. Fortunately, reality was not nearly as dramatic as fantasy. I somehow managed

Walking, Talking, Debating and Arguing with God

to direct my focus straight ahead of my path. I could almost deny the presence of people by not making eye contact. If I didn't see them, maybe they didn't see me.

Safely inside the ballroom, I planted myself on a seat. I had arrived early so there were only a few scattered people sitting and talking quietly. Then much to my relief I saw the face of someone I knew. It was the precious face of Jan. She had not been able to attend the prayer group meetings, but was here for the seminar. This was a delightful surprise. Certainly, Jan must have been my reward for making it this far instead of sneaking back to my car and driving home.

We had not seen each other in several months and had lots of catching up to do. We were both anxious to share God's blessings with one another. If nothing else happened during this three-day seminar, I was blessed to have spent time with such a saint of God. My anxiety from earlier was worth every second as she shared how the Holy Spirit had been moving in her life.

Jan had gained strength and boldness in the Lord since I had last spoken with her. She had recently been an inspiration and hope to someone who desperately needed the love of Christ. God had sent a woman who was hopelessly lost, and hungry for Jesus, into Jan's life. He was using Jan as the instrument through which His light could pierce the darkness that had overshadowed this woman's world.

After relating her inspiring story, Jan asked what I had been doing these past several months. I confessed

Command Performance

that I had mostly been arguing with God. He asks me to do something and my heart wants to, but my brain is just too scared to take the first step.

The hardest thing He's ever asked me to do, *so* far, is dance in worship before Him.

As a result of gentle, but firm, persuasion from the Holy Spirit, I gave up the fight. I learned dance steps to the song, "Shout to the Lord," and performed it for my church on Mother's Day.

As I shared with Jan my recent experience, her eyes filled with tears of joy. She knew me well enough to know my actions had to have been divinely inspired. She had no doubt God had dragged me kicking and screaming the whole way.

Together we laughed at the foolishness of humans and marveled at the patience of God. Our visitation ended after praying for each other and believing for even greater testimonies to share the next time.

With seconds remaining before the opening of the seminar, the musicians gathered on stage. People filed in looking for the best seat in the house. Every seat had a sheet of paper containing the lyrics of the evening's music selection for our convenience. Being completely unfamiliar with any of the songs, I appreciated this considerate detail.

After singing the last scheduled song, the praise leader took the microphone. He commented on the awesome presence of the Lord that had settled in the room. He said he felt in his spirit the need to sing one more song.

Walking, Talking, Debating and Arguing with God

Upon being informed of the change of schedule, the praise team began to play. The instrumental opening of the song sounded familiar, but I didn't quite recognize it. When the first words were sung, it hit me. They were singing "Shout to the Lord."

Of all the billions of songs in the world, why did they sing "Shout to the Lord"? If I hadn't shown up tonight they probably would have sung "Amazing Grace" or some other time-honored classic.

It was obvious to me that many people in the room were blessed as they listened to this song. I, on the other hand, felt something quite different. The more they sang, the more unbelievably uncomfortable I became. More than just the palms of my hands were sweating as my entire body trembled. There was actually a bead of perspiration slowly dripping down the back of my right knee. Every breath became a struggle. The thunderous pounding of my heart soon drowned out the sounds from the stage.

Emotions were racing through me with incredible speed. I felt sick, nervous, scared, and honestly, angry. I took that choice of song extremely personally, and I blamed God. How could He do this to me? I had been so obedient through all the events leading up to this seminar. I had prayed every single day for its success. I put up flyers and invited people to come. I even resisted all temptations of going home and un-volunteering to help. After everything I'd done for God, this was the thanks I got.

Command Performance

The unfortunate people sitting next to me must have thought I was suffering from some form of mental disorder. I'm afraid I may have been verbally expressing my displeasure to God while they were trying to savor His Holy presence. Growing up I wasn't a rebellious child toward my parents. I have no idea why I'm such a rebellious adult toward my Heavenly Father.

Just as the song says, I wanted to shout to the Lord. I wanted to shout, "This isn't fair"! It wasn't fair for God to ask me to dance. Not here! I explained to Him that there were far too many people. I reminded Him of some of the special guests in attendance. There were musicians, singers, and actors who were known all over the world. There was probably at least one professional dancer who could tell I'd never taken a dance class. God has a sense of humor. Maybe this was a joke. If it was, I didn't think it was very funny.

It occurred to me that I had argued long enough that the song had ended. Feeling relieved and somewhat coy, I made a deal with God. If this song were sung again during the seminar, I would dance.

I can't express my feelings when the leader of the praise team opened his mouth to sing the song a second time. No more arguing, I was even more frightened than before. Only this time, the fear of disobeying God was far greater than the fear of being embarrassed.

I was sitting on the end of a row but there was a television camera set up in the aisle next to me. So, I had to slide past the entire length of people to reach

Walking, Talking, Debating and Arguing with God

the other aisle. Mary Linda was sitting in the last seat I came to. When she asked where I was going, I told her, "Down front." My answer must have shocked her because she said, "Why?" All I could say was, "I have to dance this time."

My brain still could not believe that my feet were actually carrying my body down to stand in front of all these people. Not just stand in front of them, but dance. When I turned around to face the audience, the light blinded me. For a moment, time stood still. I couldn't see the people nor hear the music. Closing my eyes, I humbly asked to be forgiven for my disobedience. And offered praise for God's undying patience.

My will was broken. Now I stood in complete surrender. However willing, I was absolutely unable to move. The eyes of the crowd were burning into my flesh. They were waiting for me to do something. Tearfully, I asked God to enable me to do whatever He desired. If He wanted me to stand there all night and cry, I could do that. Aloud I prayed, "God if you want me to dance, let my steps be your steps. Let me dance with you."

As that prayer left my lips, the sound of the music once again spilled into my consciousness. My body fell naturally into rhythm as if by instinct. This was only the fourth time I'd ever performed this dance. Yet, remarkably, I felt no need to concentrate on my movements. I closed my eyes and offered my body as a living sacrifice to my Creator.

Command Performance

As I danced, I entered a higher realm of praise. The Holy Spirit had ushered me into the Holy of Holies. I knew I was doing more than dancing before a crowd of people. I was dancing before the Lord. Tears streamed down my face as my steps followed His divine lead. While in His glorious presence, God had taken my hand and was dancing with me.

From the Mouth of Babes

In Sunday school Jessica learned of the fruits of the spirit, and how Christians should bear fruit. Jessica's mom was dating a man who attended church on occasion. One day, Jessica's mom asked her what she thought about this man. Jessica answered, "I am going to pray for him because I think his fruit is dead."

Chapter Eight

STRETCHES, SIT-UPS, AND WEIGHTS

October 31, 1999

Today is the last day of the Bible conference. The past three days have been a wonderful growing experience for me. Now, I lie in my bed excited but exhausted from the week's events. I'm the type of person who can sleep just about anywhere, any time. Seldom do I have to wait longer than ten minutes for my trusted companion, sleep, to visit me. This is one of those rare occasions.

My body is tired but my brain is running full speed ahead. I'm thinking about what a changed person I've become since God has been working on me. I'm continually amazed at His perseverance and patience. Sometimes I think I'm more trouble than I am worth. Good thing God doesn't think so. Just like a good father, He knows my potential and refuses to give up on me.

I've asked Him to take me beyond my comfort zone and He has obliged. He's been steadily stretching me for some time. That may sound like a harmless experience. But let me tell you, it's uncomfortable.

I thought that as an adult I would no longer experience growing pains. On the contrary, I've grown more over the past three years than in the forty years prior. My growth has been more spiritual than physical, but nevertheless accompanied by intense growing pains.

I liken it to participating in a vigorous exercise program after being sedentary for years. A good exercise trainer will push you to your limit. He will train you to strengthen and build muscles you didn't know existed. At first your body aches, making the slightest movements painful. But if you're faithful and exercise religiously, rewards will follow.

Positive changes begin to take place. Your improved blood circulation brings new color to your face. Freely flowing endorphins enhance your mental and emotional well-being. Your new strengthened body lifts your posture as well as your self-esteem. Then one day others begin to notice the changes.

Stretches, Sit-ups, and Weights

Friends and family comment on the new you. They see you aren't the same as before, and they want to know your secret.

Recently, I asked God to be my personal trainer, my personal spiritual trainer that is. Graciously accepting me into His program, He wasted no time in scheduling my individualized exercise routine. Because of my sedentary spiritual lifestyle as a pew warmer, I had to start slowly.

God had to train me in the art of flexibility. He started me on a light warm-up routine of sit-ups. I was required to sit up closer to the front in church. After I was sufficiently warmed up, it was time for stretching. My first stretching exercise was a lesson in submission. This routine consisted of stretching my hands toward heaven while in God's presence. This proved more difficult than anticipated. Feeling terribly awkward I struggled to lift one hand at a time. Eventually I gained the strength to stretch them both heavenward without pain. It took over a year for me to master this exercise. The Bible tells us to offer a "sacrifice of praise." While man looks on our outward appearance, God looks at our heart. He knew this simple act was truly a sacrifice of praise I brought to His altar.

After much practice, the warm-up and stretching routines became painless. Little did I know that my training was about to step up to a higher level. God wanted me to do something more strenuous than sitting, standing, and raising my hands. He added weight

Walking, Talking, Debating and Arguing with God

lifting to my routine. Our church was trying to start a children's ministry on Wednesday evenings and we needed a teacher. My personal trainer recommended I plant my feet firmly and lift that weight. Of course I didn't jump right on that idea. Rather, I attempted to reason my way out of the situation.

I tried a logical approach when submitting my argument. Why doesn't a parent of one of these kids start this class? It doesn't make sense that I should be the one to volunteer for this job. My daughter is grown. I have no kids who would benefit from such a class. I kept hoping someone would desire to start up this ministry. Then perhaps God would find something more suitable for me. That didn't happen.

For two years I ran from this responsibility. I was comfortable with my current routine. So I pretended not to know God had called me. In reality I felt incompetent to take on such a task. This was more weight than I felt capable of handling. I couldn't understand why God would ask me to take such a giant step. I expected to start light, having heavier weights added slowly. To be entrusted with the spiritual training of young children would be an extreme responsibility, requiring great commitment. It would be a huge weight to lift.

One day I realized my spiritual growth had become stagnant over the last several months. I asked God what had happened to my workout training. In my heart I knew the answer. God was waiting for me to take on

Stretches, Sit-ups, and Weights

the task at hand before I could move on. The more I ignored His voice, the louder He spoke. His call began to interrupt my sleep. Many nights I dreamed that the children of my church were in class on Wednesday evenings listening to my teaching. I was awakened one Saturday night due to another such dream. Weary from this two-year battle, I put up the white flag. "God," I prayed, "if this is what you want, I give up. But I have to know its you. Prove it to me. Give me a sign. If I'm absolutely convinced it's you, then I'll do it."

The very next morning in church I received my sign. It was literally written out in black and white. Along the top of our bulletin in big, black, bold letters were the words "**CHILDRENS' MINISTRY LEADER NEEDED.**" I quickly closed the bulletin, waited a couple seconds, and slowly opened it again. It still read the same. I was convinced. This not-so-subtle sign was the proof I'd asked for. I walked directly over to Monica, my pastor's wife. With a shaky voice I said, "I need to teach that class." Her sweet face glowed with excitement and she replied, "Oh Robin I'm so glad you want to do this." Feeling the need to be completely honest with her I answered, "No, no I didn't say I wanted to, I said I need to." I didn't give her time to respond. For fear of changing my mind, I simply turned around and walked away.

The most difficult part of this new addition to my workout routine was the initial commitment. Once I took the step of faith, the role of teacher came naturally.

Walking, Talking, Debating and Arguing with God

There are tremendous responsibilities, but the rewards have been far greater than my expectations. As a teacher, I've learned many wonderful lessons and enjoyed tremendous growth.

My two-year dry spell came to a productive end as I became more involved in my church's activities. I joined our women's ministry group, and on occasion opened my home for special events. For the first time in my life I participated in Christian activities outside of my church, attending conventions and retreats in other cities.

God began to introduce more exciting exercises into my training program. A desire developed in me to become a blessing to my church. Selfishly, in the past, I had expected to receive blessings without giving in return. Seeking creative ways to use my talents, I designed and created banners for our sanctuary. Taking photos and videos of special services, I've attempted to document our church history.

My spiritual training had become increasingly enjoyable. Most of the painful stretching seemed to be behind me. Being faithful to this exercise routine had transformed me into a stronger person. Daily Bible reading and prayer kept me pumped and healthy. After lots of hard work, I was satisfied with my spiritual fitness. Following the instructions of my Personal Trainer I had reached my goal.

However, the goals we set for ourselves are seldom as high as those set by God. This revelation came to me

Stretches, Sit-ups, and Weights

quite abruptly one spring day during a retreat in the Smokey Mountains. The message I received from God caught me completely off guard. He told me that I had not received an answer to a particular prayer because I was holding my gifts from Him.

I honestly had no idea what He meant. I thought I was doing everything right. As a matter of fact, I discussed that very subject with Him. I read down my list of spiritual accomplishments. He didn't flinch. Instead, He said, "I put dance in your step, but you don't use it for my kingdom. You need to dance in worship before me."

Needless to say, I wasn't exactly thrilled with this news. I had asked for spiritual training for the strength to speak. I wanted spiritual wisdom to fill my mouth. For years I'd prayed for God to give me words, but never movement. In my younger days I prayed for God to bless me, but only on my terms. My hands would remain relaxed at my sides, not raised in the air. I preferred not to shed tears because my makeup would run. Stammering lips were definitely out of the question. Above all else I wanted to remain standing. Under no circumstances would I be willing to fall under the power of the Holy Spirit. I wanted to sit in my pew, receive a blessing, and then leave quietly after service without anyone noticing me.

My spiritual training has brought me a long way since those days. I no longer worry about tears ruining my makeup. Since I cry at the slightest move of God, I

Walking, Talking, Debating and Arguing with God

simply stopped wearing mascara on my bottom lashes. Whenever the Holy Spirit shows up in a service and overpowers people's ability to stand, the odds are pretty good I will be among those lying on the carpet. I've even grown to the point of possessing a heavenly prayer language. As described in the book of Acts, I have received the gift of speaking in tongues.

But now dancing, that was a different story. I wanted God to stretch me, but this was much further than I wanted to go. This was not part of my plan. My plan was to be a verbal witness, not a physical one. After hearing this message from God, I basically threw a tantrum. I acted like a spoiled child who didn't get her way. I argued. I cried. I pouted. I even sought counsel from my pastor's wife in hopes she would help me find a way out. In the end, I obeyed, reluctantly, but nevertheless, I obeyed.

Since I first asked God to take me out of my comfort zone, He has stretched me beyond what I thought possible. He has tested my limits, but rewarded me with blessings as each test was completed. My spiritual strength endured a series of such tests during this Bible conference. I was put through vigorous exercise routines at the hand of my Personal Trainer.

Following the pattern of my training, the routines started with sit-ups and stretches. Being a volunteer prayer partner for the conference, I was required to sit up close to the platform. The first two rows of seats were reserved for us. During specific times in the conference,

Stretches, Sit-ups, and Weights

people were asked to stand if they had particular prayer needs. We prayer partners were instructed to stretch our hands toward them and agree in prayer for victory.

Of course there's no better way to build strength than with a weight-lifting routine. Ironically, the weight of teaching, which took me over two years to lift during training, was the easiest for me now. I was teaching people about faith and obedience just by sharing my testimony. On several occasions I had the opportunity to teach on God's patience and faithfulness using myself as an example. In prayer meetings and during breaks at the seminar, we would share with one another some of His wonderful blessings. Just like teaching my class on Wednesday nights, I learned as much, if not more, than I taught.

The most difficult part of my training was the praise dancing. It just goes against everything I've been taught my whole life. Dancing was done in bars and nightclubs. Such unholy activity was a direct ticket to hell. Yet God has told me to dance in worship before Him. It's been almost a year since my first dance steps in obedience to this command. I'm able to dance in front of my own church body on Sundays without hyperventilating, but it's still difficult. If God would as much as hint that I no longer needed to be in this form of ministry, I would never take another step.

Because of the extreme difficulty of this particular exercise, I never expected to be tested on it during this conference. I'm not good enough at it. My lack of

Walking, Talking, Debating and Arguing with God

strength and form in this routine is obvious. I need more training and more practice. Lots more practice.

The Bible tells us God's ways are not our ways. His thoughts are not our thoughts. This Scripture came to life for me during this conference. God expected me to do something completely beyond my capability. He told me to dance in worship before Him and everybody in that conference. I wasn't worried about what He would think. He had already seen me dance. It was everybody else that made me nervous.

The decision of my personal trainer to have me perform this exercise made no sense. I couldn't figure out the purpose of dancing in front of all those strangers. The very thought caused my muscles to weaken with fear. I may not be able to stand, let alone dance. My trembling body would be distracting if I did make an attempt. Who could possibly receive a blessing from this?

It's not my place to question the motives of my Creator. So, I stopped trying to understand God's thought pattern. I made the difficult decision to just shut up and obey. After praying for and receiving strength, I performed a praise dance.

As I danced in obedience to Him, it all began to make sense. That's when I realized who would be blessed from this. I would. God was trying to hand me a blessing. And in return I was upset about having to do something I didn't think was fair. This was the toughest test of the conference, but with it came the greatest blessing.

Stretches, Sit-ups, and Weights

That night I tossed and turned in bed waiting for my mind to tire. After mentally reliving my Christian walk for hours, my brain finally started to slow down and feel sleepy. Just before allowing me to rest, one last thought entered my consciousness. I concluded that no matter how unlovable I am, God loves me. Regardless of how much I argue and rebel, He waits for, and accepts, my apology. And though I've acted extremely ungrateful at times, He continues to give me gifts.

Feeling somewhat ashamed of my actions, I fell asleep with a spirit of conviction. As I slept God revealed something to me in a dream. In this dream I saw the tiny fragile arm of a child. Because of the snowy white skin with the exception of one distinct freckle, I recognized it as being the arm of my five-year-old granddaughter, Jimi.

Stretching forward, her arm turned over facing palm up. Her hand was opened flat as if waiting to have something placed in it. Next my arm came into the picture. Reaching out, I placed a quarter into her hand. Her fingers quickly closed around the coin holding it tight.

As she turned away her entire image came into view. Soft brown curls danced across her back as she skipped and hopped over to a line of bubble gum machines. One machine contained big bright candy balls. Another housed small square colorful gum pieces. The third machine was filled with clear plastic bubbles. Inside each bubble was a toy. For the price of one quarter a wide variety of toys were available. However, the machine had control over which toy would be selected.

Choosing between candy, gum, or an undetermined toy can be quite a challenge when you're five. Important choices such as this require careful consideration. Not reacting hastily, Jimi studied the situation, weighing all her options. After several minutes she made the decision of which machine would receive her coin. The clear plastic bubbles had captured her interest. Through the glass, she surveyed the different toys safely secured in their own bubble. The various possibilities intrigued her.

Putting the quarter into the slot, Jimi tried to turn the handle. Her little fingers strained until her knuckles were white. But the cold metal handle didn't budge. Seeing her struggle, I reached down and placed my hand on top of hers. Together the two of us turned the handle to release a surprise toy packed in a bubble.

Familiar sounds from the machine caused excitement to build within her. The metal handle clicked as it turned. Churning mechanisms caused the enticing bubbles to move. The subtle sound of plastic tapping against plastic could be heard as the bubbles tumbled and rolled over each other. Intently she listened to the sound of plastic against metal as one fateful bubble entered the exit chamber.

Both of her hands were now cupped directly below the trap door from which the prize would be retrieved.

Stretches, Sit-ups, and Weights

By the time the selected bubble hit the door she was literally bouncing with enthusiasm. Her eyes sparkled with delight.

Once the bubble came to rest against the door she didn't immediately reach for it as I expected. Instead she asked me what I thought the toy might be. I knew she would have loved for it to be a lovely ring with a pink "diamond." However, I also knew she'd be happy with whatever happened to be hidden behind the door. She had no idea what tiny trinket awaited her, yet she was overwhelmed with anticipation. It didn't matter to her which prize she had received. What mattered was that she had received a gift.

The content of this dream was more reality than fantasy. Jimi is as grateful for a yo-yo that never comes back up after it drops the first time as she is with one of the cherished pink rings. She doesn't question motives or show signs of disappointment. At five years old, she knows how to graciously accept a gift. She smiles, says thank you, and offers a heartfelt hug.

Not surprisingly, I woke from my dream before the prize was revealed. But of course the identity of the toy wasn't the issue. The lesson God had for me in this dream was not missed. Even through the fog of sleep, the message rang loud and clear. His Word says we are to come unto Him as a child.

God used my granddaughter to teach me an important lesson. I learned that maturity doesn't automatically come with age. Usually when God tries to move in my life, I display more defiance than a five-year-old child does. My first reaction is to whine and argue, questioning His decisions concerning my life. Most of the time I want to know why, before I obey. As if He owes me any explanation for anything ever!

Such immature actions come from having the trust and faith of an adult. If I possessed the maturity of a child, I would trust totally. My faith would be unshakable. It would enable me to accept God's gifts without question. Even the tiniest trinket from above would cause me to bounce with enthusiasm.

As a child I liked surprises. As an adult they make me nervous. There's comfort in knowing what lies ahead. I can plan around the expected, and maintain control. Unexpected surprises tend to mess up my plans. They make me lose my sense of security. God showed me in this dream that he has many surprises for my life. He has told me not to fear the unexpected. When it becomes impossible for me to go on alone, He will put His hand over mine. Together we will turn the handle that releases His blessing.

Our Heavenly Father has an array of colorful gifts for all of us. These gifts are free. All the quarters in the world can't buy even the smallest one. However, control of which gift will drop into the exit chamber belongs to the Lord. We may have our eye on the pink diamond, or the spy ring, and get the yo-yo instead. Nevertheless, we should be genuinely overwhelmed with anticipation upon receiving anything from Him.

Every gift, anointing, blessing, and unexpected surprise should be accepted with excitement and enthusiasm. My desire is to grow to the maturity of a child. To accept anything God hands me with a smile, a thank you, and a heartfelt hug.

From the Mouth of Babes

Heidi: "Thank you Jesus for my *coolness*."

Walking, Talking, Debating and Arguing with God Order Form

Postal orders: 2471 Callis Road
Lebanon, TN 37090

Telephone orders: 615-449-3124

E-mail orders: RobinHardin.com

Please send *Walking, Talking, Debating and Arguing with God* **to:**

Name: _____

Address: _____

City: _____ State: _____

Zip: _____

Telephone: (____) _____

Book Price: $10.00

Shipping: $3.00 for the first book and $1.00 for each additional book to cover shipping and handling within US, Canada, and Mexico. International orders add $6.00 for the first book and $2.00 for each additional book.

Or order from:
ACW Press
5501 N. 7th. Ave. #502
Phoenix, AZ 85013

(800) 931-BOOK

or contact your local bookstore